# MY PET

# Guinea Pig

Honor Head

Photographs by
Jane Burton

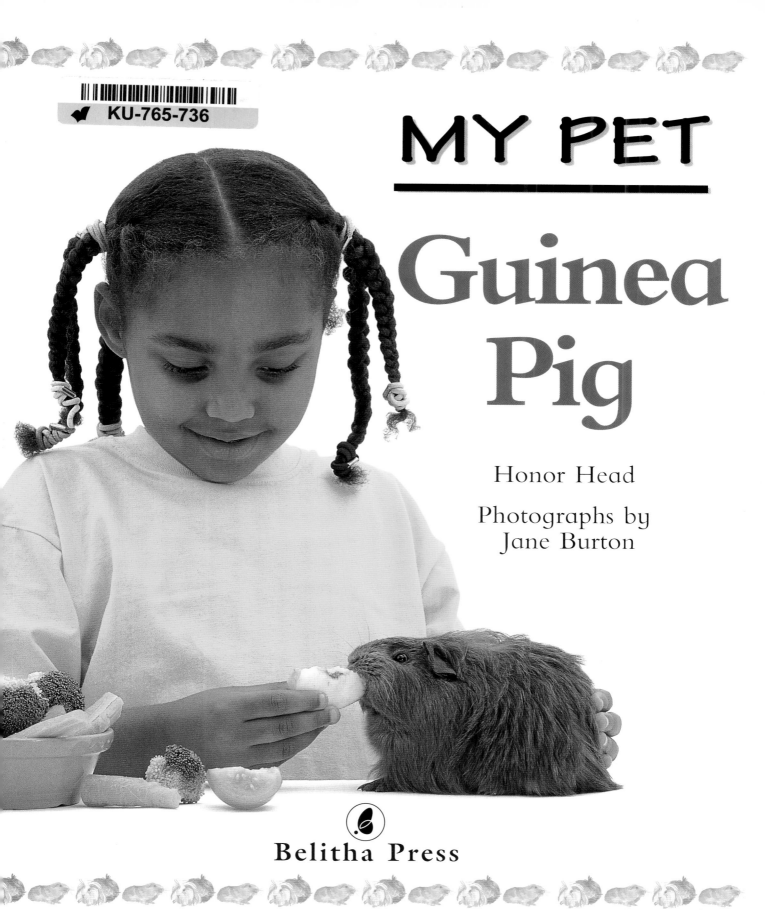

Belitha Press

First published in the UK in 2000 by
Belitha Press
A member of Chrysalis Books plc
64 Brewery Road, London N7 9NT

Paperback edition first published in 2003.

ISBN 1 84138 112 8 (hardback)
ISBN 1 84138 353 8 (paperback)

British Library Cataloguing in Publication Data
for this book is available from the
British Library.

Editor: Claire Edwards
Designer: Rosamund Saunders
Illustrator: Pauline Bayne
Consultant: Frazer Swift

Printed in Hong Kong

10 9 8 7 6 5 4 3 2 1 (hb)
10 9 8 7 6 5 4 3 2 1 (pb)

PDSA (People's Dispensary for Sick
Animals) is Britain's largest charity which
each year provides free treatment for some
1.4 million sick and injured animals of
disadvantaged owners.

A royalty of 2.5 per cent of the proceeds from
this book will be paid to the PDSA (People's
Dispensary for Sick Animals) on every copy
sold in the UK.

The products featured have been kindly
donated by Pets at Home.

# Contents

# My guinea pig

ear

whiskers

coat

claws

# It's fun owning your own pet.

Guinea pigs make good pets and are great fun, but they need to be looked after carefully.

Your pet may be with you for a long time. Guinea pigs need feeding every day and their hutch needs to be kept clean. You must also be gentle with guinea pigs as they can be easily frightened.

Young children with pets should always be supervised by an adult. For further notes, please see page 32.

# There are many different types of guinea pigs.

Some guinea pigs have short, smooth hair, others have ruffled or long hair.

Long-haired guinea pigs are harder to look after. They need lots of grooming.

Guinea pigs need company and like to play together.

**Some guinea pigs are just one colour. Others have patches and stripes.**

A guinea pig's hair is called a coat.

# A pregnant guinea pig needs peace and quiet.

When a guinea pig is pregnant she will eat more. She will also need more water to drink.

Just before she has her babies, the mother guinea pig needs to be left alone and handled very carefully.

A guinea pig has about three babies. She licks them clean as soon as they are born.

**A pregnant guinea pig will need a little bread soaked in milk as well as her normal food.**

# Baby guinea pigs are born with all their fur.

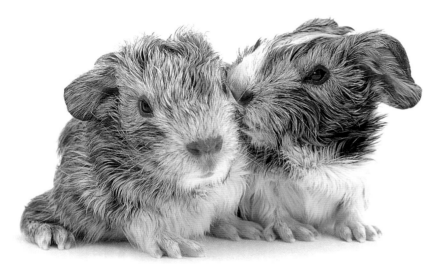

A newborn guinea pig looks like its mother. Its eyes are open and it has all its teeth.

**Baby guinea pigs suckle until they are about three weeks old. They also begin to eat solid food after one or two days.**

Newborn guinea pigs drink their mother's milk straight away. This is called suckling.

When guinea pigs are one week old they can move around quite quickly.

This baby guinea pig is three weeks old. He will be old enough to leave his mother at five weeks.

# Your guinea pig will need a warm hutch to live in.

A hutch should have one bit you can see into and one bit that is closed off, where your guinea pig can sleep.

If the hutch is outside, make sure it is sheltered from rain, wind and direct sunshine. It should be waterproof and raised off the ground. Bring it inside in cold weather.

Put a layer of newspaper at the bottom of the hutch with wood shavings on top. Put plenty of hay in the sleeping area.

Your guinea pig should have a run or ark where it can run around. Make sure the run is strong, so that it can't be knocked over.

# Your guinea pig will need time to settle in.

When you show your guinea pig its new home it may feel scared. Leave it alone for a little while until it is used to you.

Your guinea pig will enjoy exploring. Give it some toys to play with.

Cut some holes in a box for your pet to crawl through. Hide some food for it in a large flowerpot.

Your guinea pig needs to be looked after every day. If you are going on holiday, ask a friend to look after your pet. Pack everything your guinea pig will need. Carry your guinea pig in a special carrier.

# Your guinea pig will enjoy being picked up.

Always be gentle and quiet with your guinea pig. Loud noises and sudden movements will frighten it. Talk to it quietly so that it grows used to your voice.

**If your guinea pig is happy it may chirrup or purr.**

When you pick up your guinea pig, stroke it gently. Kneel down. Put one hand around the guinea pig's chest and the other hand under its bottom to lift it.

Do not squeeze your guinea pig. If it struggles put it down immediately. Never drop your guinea pig – you will hurt it. Always put it down on the ground.

# Give your guinea pig lots of nice things to eat.

Feed your guinea pig some fresh fruit and vegetables every day. Give it plenty of mixed greens, but not lettuce. Always wash fresh food carefully.

Give your pet special guinea pig food twice a day.

**Fruit and vegetables will help to keep your guinea pig healthy. You can also pick wild plants for your pet, but you need to check which kinds are safe.**

Buy your guinea pig a water bottle and keep it filled with fresh water all the time. Make sure the spout is metal, as guinea pigs chew their bottles.

# Keep your guinea pig's hutch clean.

Clean your guinea pig's hutch once a day. Take out dirty bedding and old food. Make sure the guinea pig's hay is clean and there is enough to make a cosy bed.

Clean your pet's water bottle at least once a week with a bottle brush. Wash the food bowl every day.

Scrub out the hutch once a week
with disinfectant from a pet shop.
Put in clean paper, wood shavings
and bedding. Wear rubber gloves,
or wash you hands afterwards.

**Scrub out the hutch more
often when the weather
is hot. Dry it carefully
before you put the
new bedding in.**

# Have fun looking after your guinea pig.

Brush your guinea pig's coat gently the way the fur grows with a soft brush. If your guinea pig has long or rough fur, brush it every day with a stiff brush. This is called grooming.

Guinea pigs with short hair lick themselves clean, but they still like to be groomed.

You can buy a mineral block for your guinea pig. Minerals help to keep your guinea pig healthy.

A well-fed, healthy guinea pig has silky, clean-smelling fur, bright eyes and clean ears and nose.

# Your guinea pig may need to visit the vet.

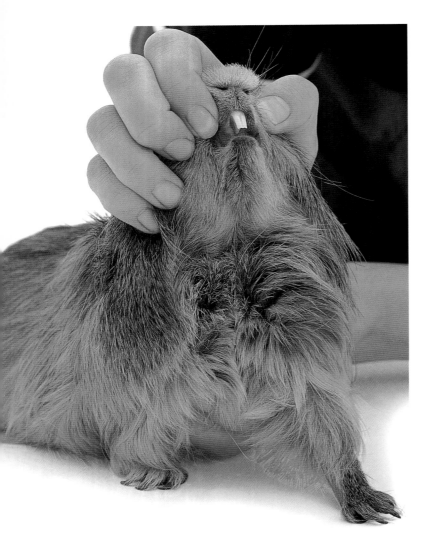

Your vet will be able to answer any questions you have about your guinea pig's health. If your pet is ill, the vet may give it some medicine. The vet may also check your pet's teeth to make sure they are not too long.

Give your guinea pig a block of wood to gnaw on. This will help to keep its front teeth sharp and not too long.

If your guinea pig's claws grow too long, your vet will clip them for you.

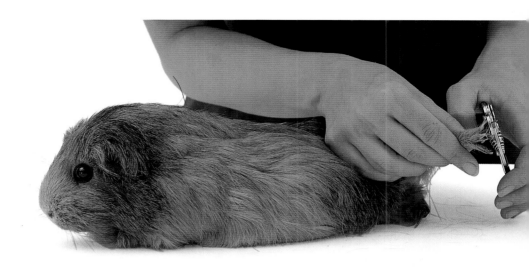

Check your pet's fur to make sure that there are no little insects in it. If there are, buy some powder from the vet. When you use the powder, cover your pet's face with one hand.

# Your guinea pig will need a friend.

Guinea pigs do not like living
alone. The best friend for your
guinea pig is another guinea pig.
Two females or two males from
the same litter will get on well.

Rabbits get on well with guinea pigs if they are introduced when they are both young.

Your guinea pig will enjoy meeting your friends. Make sure you are not too noisy when you are with your guinea pig and don't run around with it.

# Your guinea pig may live for up to seven years.

As your guinea pig grows old make especially sure it is kept warm. Check your guinea pig every day, especially its ears, eyes and nose. Call your vet if you are worried about anything.

**As your guinea pig grows older it will sleep more and play less.**

Guinea pigs usually live for about five years. Like people they grow old and die. You may feel sad when this happens but you will be able to look back and remember all the happy times you had with your guinea pig.

# Words to remember

**ark** A type of large hutch where guinea pigs can run around. Also called a **run**.

**bedding** Material for your pet to sleep in.

**coat** The name for a guinea pig's fur.

**groom** To brush an animal's fur to keep it clean.

**hutch** A wooden house where pets such as guinea pigs live.

**mineral block** A special type of food for your guinea pig.

**puppy** A baby guinea pig.

**suckling** When a baby guinea pig drinks its mother's milk it is suckling.

**vet** An animal doctor.

## Newborn guinea pigs are like tiny adults.

Newborn.

One week old.

Three weeks old.

# Index

# Notes for parents

Guinea pigs make excellent pets and will give you and your family a great deal of pleasure. But keeping any animal is a big responsibility. If you decide to buy guinea pigs for your child, you will need to ensure that they are healthy, happy and safe. You will also have to care for them if they are ill and supervise your child with them until he or she is at least five years old. It is your responsibility to make sure your child does not harm the guinea pigs and learns to handle them correctly.

Here are some other points to think about before you decide to own a guinea pig:

* Do you have somewhere to keep your guinea pigs out of draughts and not in direct sunshine?

* Guinea pigs can live for up to seven years. You may have to pay vet's bills if they are ill.

* If you go on holiday, you will need to make sure someone can care for the guinea pigs while you are away.

* Do you have other pets? Will the guinea pigs get on with them? Cats and dogs will usually frighten guinea pigs. Keep them apart.

* You should never keep a guinea pig on its own. Males from the same litter can be kept together, as can females from the same litter. Don't keep males and females together as this will result in unwanted litters.

* Guinea pigs fed on the latest complete diets should not be fed mineral supplements unless specifically advised by a vet.

This book is intended as an introduction only for young readers. If you have any queries about how to look after your pet guinea pig, you can contact the PDSA (People's Dispensary for Sick Animals) at Whitechapel Way, Priorslee, Telford, Shropshire TF2 9PQ. Tel: 01952 290999.